About the Author

Tucker Merrihew is a successful entrepreneur and Real Estate Investor who has been active in the Portland Oregon Real Estate Market for over ten years. His company, TTM Development Company, has been flipping, wholesaling and building homes since 2009. His podcast, **The Real Dealz Podcast**, was first released in January of 2014 and has gathered a large following worldwide. Listeners tune in every week for an in-depth, highly knowledgeable and candid picture of Real Estate Investing. Follow Tucker's Podcast and BLOG at www.therealdealzpodcast.com.

Tucker has also created **The Deal Finders Academy**, which is an REI Mastermind group of the best investors in the country. Tucker is currently working on his **Negotiating with Sellers** product, which will teach investors the best strategies for negotiating directly with homeowners to get the best deals possible.

Table of Contents

You Saw What Exactly?

When I first began to invest in Real Estate, I was confident I knew what I was doing. I had listened to countless GURU's who told me I could be rich within a very short time of flipping POS houses, driving hundred thousand dollar sports cars, sun tanning on luxury yachts and, of course, I could have some bombshell blonde babe as my arm candy. All of this, simply because I was a "Real Estate Investor." From the outside, the business seemed glamorous, as if I could become a rock star for the ordinary every day guy. I soaked up every bit of information I could get my eyes and ears on, and at some point, I felt like I really knew the Real Estate Investing business and how this getting rich flipping houses thing worked.

When I started, I knew how to value a property. I knew about real estate financing since I had spent the previous six years selling money to people who wanted to buy or refinance a home. I knew the process like the back of my hand from actually having bought a house. I really felt like I knew what I was doing and what I was about to get myself into. But, did I really know what I was walking into? Sure, I thought. How hard could this really be? Buy a house at 50 cents on the dollar and then resell it at

100cents, right? But what I didn't know, and what no GURU ever talked about, is who really lives in the homes that I would want to flip. What would I see when venturing into the world of dilapidated and torn up homes? I mean, did I even know who lived in these homes? To be honest, I had no idea. Not a damn clue. I could easily value these homes on paper, sure, but what about the inside of these homes? What about the people with whom I would deal with? What about the amount of work those homes would need? These were questions I hadn't considered and no GURU had ever talked about. That was a whole other world.

To establish some context, understand that I take Chris, my office manager and listing agent, on all my appointments to look at a potential home for sale. We book these appointments through a lot of direct mail to distressed or dilapidated homes, and those owners will call in. We will then work with the seller to see inside the home and then potentially purchase the home for a discount. Why a discount you may ask? Weed, meth, hoarding and a variety of other things that no child should ever see (or adult for that matter). The homes are destroyed from bad habits and just nasty living. I'm serious, this is just the start. Anyone who says Real Estate Investors are taking advantage of people by purchasing their homes at 50 cents on the dollar, I would ask them to spend a day with Chris and I touring these homes. Or, at the very least, read this book!

Take, for example, the time we met a probate attorney at an old, distressed home some of her clients were trying to liquidate from their parent's estate. It's not in too bad a shape, she said. I remember my hesitation. I thought if it's not in too bad of shape, then it's probably not in bad enough shape for us to get the home at the price we want. Well, I was wrong. The home had giant sections of siding missing with baseball size openings on those pieces still attached.

Eventually we discovered the sub flooring was exposed in most areas and was also missing planks, so that you could see all the way through to the crawl space (which was filled with crap, debris and almost certainly a large number of varmints). I was waiting for us to stumble across a large hole in the ground with a skin suit at the bottom. The weirdest part was the door we were trying to access the home through. It had been tied shut with a mangy piece of rope and even then, the inside of the door was barricaded by nasty old mattresses and other bed bug infested furniture! By the time we finally crawled in through a back window, we found some lights on and some very, very odd music playing.

"I thought you said it was empty," I asked the probate attorney.

You know what she said? "Well, it should be." As you can imagine I got the hell out of that place as quickly as my two feet move.

There was also the home with rotting food on the counter and piles of cat shit littered every 6 inches in the entire home. There was the home that had 4 or 5 additions, none of which were permitted. It was like a maze at the Willy Wonka chocolate factory and an endless optical illusion. The ceiling kept getting lower and the doors kept getting smaller, and by the end, I was almost on my hands and knees to go inside a room that was too small to even live in. Or, most recently, there was the lady who bought the house next door and had a contractor build an illegal hallway that linked one home to the other. It didn't make sense. It was just her and her cats and both homes were in complete disrepair and were falling apart virtually right in front of our eyes. Bizarre and surreal would have been an understatement. I mean, what was the point?

What you have to understand is this: these homes are in such disrepair that the owners couldn't sell them to someone who would move in and live there even if they wanted to! Who is going to buy a home in which a wall in the master bedroom is covered with black mold?

Sure, you can clean it off. Maybe even bleach it. But what about all the moisture and rot going on inside the walls that is still under the surface. So, in a way, our job is to offer a service (as unglamorous as it really is). We buy a home for a steep discount and maybe we renovate, or rehabilitate the home. Sometimes, we tear out most of the walls and gut the house. Other times, we tear the whole damn thing down and just rebuild. I mean, if the home has sewage pooling on the bathroom and basement floor, and the owners don't want to be responsible for their own home repairs, we might as well buy it from them at a discount, clean up the disgusting mess, make the necessary repairs, and fix the root of the problem. By the way, we've faced this exact issue. The smell will hit you like your first gut punch on the playground. Bam! You can't breathe. What do you do? Well for a seasoned Real Estate Pro.....You act like it's almost normal and put on your poker face. Sure, we can fix that no problem. Cough. Cough.

There are these stories, there are others and there will always be more. For now, though, we're going to look at the craziest stuff I've seen over the last five years. Remember, this is just my path down the road of Real Estate Investing. Keep your mind open. It might get weird in here. I promise, this isn't fiction. I don't think I could even imagine most of these stories if I tried.

Lord of the Undies

<u>Snapshot</u>:

There is no proper way to begin the story about this house. The dealings with these "owners" are as worthless as the house. Why? It has to do with the time and the place of the home and the people. It's hard to say where the deal started, but I know this: there were two brothers who had inherited a house in southeast Portland. One brother lived in the house (we'll call him "Bob") and the other brother lived in Florida (we'll call him "Jim"). We found out about the house from Jim. Somehow, one of our marketing pieces had made its way across the country.

Now, understand, Jim seemed perfectly normal on the phone. There was no reason to believe we would see anything that odd. Also, he hadn't seen the home in recent years. How long? Long enough to have no idea what sort of disrepair and disgust the home had become. It was like a Mad Max vision. Or better yet, like a scene prop from the TV show, The Walking Dead. And it took some back-and-forth between Jim and his brother to let us into the house.

At first, Bob told Jim that anyone who tried to enter would be bludgeoned to death on sight. We thought he was joking. He wasn't. Later, we found out Bob is crazy, just not that kind of crazy. So, Chris tried calling Bob himself and from there, Chris was able to sweet talk Bob into letting us inside to take a look. We were excited. We hadn't been investing that long. We thought, This is a golden opportunity! In its own way, it was golden. Maybe not much of an opportunity.

Chris and I pulled into the "driveway" and the first thing we see in the front yard is a picnic table turned upside down. Why? Don't ask. I didn't. Debris was everywhere, as well as random piles of ashen charcoal. Yellow weeds were up to my knees. My first thought had to do with the "For Sale" sign across the street. *Who is going to buy that house if they have to look at this every day?*

Regardless, I thought to myself, this is investing, right? You buy a pile of shit, put some money into it and then you've got a fruit salad. Well, Maybe.

The porch was a rotted resemblance of what a porch should be. The strangest part was that the porch was completely covered by shredded, blue tarps and odd cuts of plywood. No openings. No windows or screens. Just tarps and plywood. "Should we go in?" Chris asked.

I shrugged. "Yeah. Why not?"

"Well," Chris said, and motioned towards the porch. "Where is the opening? I mean, how the hell do you get to the front door?"

That was when I noticed the tarps covered the entrance, too. As we got closer, we noticed the porch steps were covered with a pile of random junk. I turned to Chris, and said, "No wonder."

We did find a way in. A small slit was cut through one side of the tarp and you had to fold the flaps up and crawl inside. What we crawled into was a hoarder's paradise. Just piles and piles of junk. We stood and made our way through a valley of trash to the door.

We expected Bob to answer, but he didn't. A pear-shaped woman with thick, brown hair answered and let us know she was Bob's wife. The inside was no different than the outside, save for the fact that it was worse. The junk was piled as high as our heads. In real terms, floor to roof was glass bottles, newspapers, old cigarette cartons, and much more. "They're collectibles," she said, and reached for a 7-Up bottle. It was plastic, and there was still moisture trapped inside, like she had drank it last week. Sure, I saw some old, yellow newspapers but they weren't The Oregonian or anything. They were newsletters for the neighborhood and stuff like that. "Nice," I said. "Could we see the rest of the house?"

And we did. One at time, we had to shuffle through the valley of rotting debris. I knew all this crap could topple. It could crush my chest. I'm going to die for a god damn deal! I thought.

So, I braced myself and stayed alert for the landslide. It was so dark and dank inside, I felt like Moses parting the god damn Red Sea. Bc ready, I wanted to tell Chris. When the time comes, we fight!

The first bedroom was scuzzy and wrecked and full of more "collectibles." It wasn't anything different from the rest of the house. The bathroom, though, was a mess of things I can't explain. The scent was a brick to the face. It hurt my lungs to breathe. Toilet water pooled across the floor. Mold had become a decorative addition to the wall paper. As I studied the bathroom, and Chris asked her a few simple questions, I noticed clothes hanging off the shower pole. An old shirt. A pair of tube socks. A pair of underwear. They weren't Bob's underwear. They were Bob's wife's underwear. And they weren't her everyday underwear. They were her *That time of the month* underwear. A white cotton Pair fading to yellow. They had a big pink stain where a big pink stain should be bleached out. It was too much. "Oh," I said. "I see there is no fan."

"No," she said. "No fan."

"That's why you have an issue with the mold."

"Mold?" she said. "What mold?"

I shrugged, then smiled by best smile of forgiveness. What was I going to say? No mold! The mold was everywhere! It was a fungus on a funeral march that had swallowed the bath tub! What was I supposed to do? "How about upstairs?" I asked. And pushed my way towards the stairs.

Generally, stairs are just stairs. You go up, then you go down. Whatever, right? In this house a stair was just another word for "shelf." That's right. More crap. More crap stacked everywhere.

So, I ascend the stairs first, then Chris follows. It's a steeper staircase. It's also a bit narrow. So, when you get to the top, there is a half wall that opens up into a top floor that has the shape of a non-conforming space, but it is up to code. I don't know what else to say but that the angles were off, it was dark, and I couldn't see. That's why I jumped at the top of the stairs. That's why I was startled.

Just on the other side of that half-wall at the top of the stairs, I noticed a little cubby cut out of the wall, like a dumb waiter. Watching me from that dark corner were two beady little eyes. That's what made me jump. I wasn't told anyone was up here. "Hello?" I said. "Hi?"

I stepped off the stairs and stepped towards the eyes. "Hello?" I said again. I thought, what is that? Why aren't they saying anything? As Chris and I got closer, I noticed the eyes had a face and big, bright teeth and a small, crouching body in the dark. It was a boy. He was maybe 11 or 12 or 13. He was staring at us. His face arced into a sly grin as he nimbly worked away rolling cigarettes.

"Who is that?" Chris whispered. "Gollum," I said. "He's real!"

"Hey man," I said. Gollum smiled something sinister. He licked his lips a little. "I'm here to see Bob," I said. "Over here?" I pointed to a room in the back. The door was open. Gollum flicked his brow, then nodded.

Inside, I found Bob. He was lying on the bed, his short off, his skin blocked and purple. He said he couldn't get out of bed. I wondered, how would he have bludgeoned someone to death? Would his wife drag them up here? Would Gollum descend from the roof top and suck their blood? Anything was possible at this point, so I talked business with Bob.

In the end, it was pointless. He didn't know anything about anything, he simply didn't want to move. If he did, he would have had to pay rent for a place and get out of bed. This required stress, he said. A stress he shouldn't have to endure. So, I got the sob story. Then, Chris and I got the fuck out of there.

We didn't make the deal, though we wanted to try. Like I said, it was too much laziness and too much complacency. What was one to do? But skip down the stairs, passed the stained underwear, onto the porch to crawl through the slit and drive away to the next appointment…

The "Keifer" Sutherland House

<u>Snapshot</u>:

The "Keifer" Sutherland House was brought to our attention through a local probate attorney. She had been appointed the personal representative of the deceased. Why? As you will see, he had alienated his family and apparently, they wanted nothing to do with his shitty estate (This is a pun. You'll see why). This was a few years back, and at this point, the business had been churning along for a couple years. I had done a lot of wholesale projects and I had completed some renovations for the lower and middle range buyers. But, at the time, I had hoped this would be one of my first big renovations, so that I might break into the higher-end REI market.

So, that day, we had the following appointment first, then a second appointment an hour later. Both of these homes were in Alameda Ridge, which is a nice, high-end neighborhood of Portland, OR. We bought the second home and made a healthy profit. As for The "Keifer" Sutherland House, the deal didn't smell right...

Chris and I had received the referral, we set the appointment and we drove down to The "Kiefer" Sutherland House to take a look around. We thought, maybe we'll even put in a bid.

It was an old house, but from the outside it didn't look much different from any other old home. Peeling paint. An old roof. A dried up lawn. Like I said, an old home. Inside, we found out we were not the only group scouting the home that day. There are a few realtors, as well. It's not until we are inside that the Probate Attorney decides to tell us about the deceased. "He had an issue," she said. "A very unique disorder in which he collected his own urine in mason jars. There are still some jars left. In the basement." She continues to tell us the top floor was cleaned out. The basement had not been cleaned out, though. No big deal, I thought. I can get the crew to clean out the basement and then we'll gut the inside and check the rot inside the walls. I got this, I thought. What does a realtor really know about renovating a home?

"One last thing," she said. "Before I let you go." Here it is, I thought. What does she want? "Well, I-," the Probate Attorney seemed to hesitate before continuing. "I have to disclose that the deceased not only kept trash and debris and his urine in mason jars. He also bottled and collected his feces. So, I guess, watch your step."

In my mind, I'm screaming and laughing, and wondering who the hell was this guy? What line of work is this? Regardless, I kept a straight face and let the image of this man fall to the floor. Business, I had to remind myself. Business.

Chris and I took a look around. It was a mess inside. We had expected that. But the basement was gross. The mason jars were stacked and categorized on dilapidated, old shelves. I took some mental measurements and I went outside. I didn't step onto the grass. I mean, you never know? He went to the bathroom in jars, maybe he went to the bathroom outside? Sidewalk only. Porch only. Deck only. I had to be in the clear.

The house was gross, but it was a really good deal. I knew this then and I know this now. But after a few tours around the house, Chris and I chatted with the Probate Attorney about the place and said it was time to go. We would definitely put in a bid.

We had 45 minutes, maybe an hour until our next appointment. So, we drove around the area because our next appointment was only 10 or 12 blocks away. I asked Chris what he thought about the house. "That's a good deal," he said. "Gross, though. It stank. I can still smell it."

"Yeah," I said. "Me, too."

"Man, what a stink."

"Yeah," I said. "Jesus." With every turn I took towards the main road, it seemed the smell got worse. At every block, the house receded farther and farther away. I couldn't figure it out. Was there a dark cloud around us? Was the stench of The "Keifer" Sutherland House a fog that descended over the neighborhood?

"Man," Chris said. "I don't get it. It just smells."

"Chris," I said. "Did you step in something?"

"What? No."

"Come on, check your shoes." Chris crossed his right leg and checked the bottom of his shoes. Nothing, he said, and checked his left foot. Nothing. "I didn't step in shit," he said.

"Damn it, Chris," I said. "Then who did? Who stepped in it?"

"I think it's just a stench from the house."

"Check your shoes," I said. "Check them!"

"I did, damn it. I did check them!"

"Well, then, what is that smell?"

"Well," Chris said. "Did you check your shoes?"

I told Chris I didn't walk in the yard. I told Chris it couldn't be me. I didn't step in anything. Besides, the cleaning crew had cleaned out all the shit from the top floor of the house. "Yeah," Chris said. "But I don't know if they got everything in the basement."

"Oh shit," I said and swerved the car to the right. "Oh shit," I said again, and got out of the car and leaned against the hood to lift up my left foot. "God damn it!" I said. "I stepped in Sutherlands remains!"

Chris started laughing as I ran to the nearest lawn and started wiping my foot into the grass. "Get off, damn it. Get off!"

I dragged the sole of my boot into the grass again and again, but Sutherlands remains smacked deeper into the tread. "Damn it," I said. "What the hell?"

Chris kept laughing and pointing at me. "Come on," he said. "I'm sure you've got it all."

I thought I had, but I could still smell it as I got back into the car and skirted down the road towards Starbucks. What the hell? I thought. "I really stepped in it this time!" I said. Without realizing what I had said, my pun sent Chris into a hysterical fit. I raced to Starbucks and parked. I threw open the door and jumped out. I began wiping my foot in the bushes. I wiped and wiped, and screamed at Chris. "Stop laughing!" I said. "Stop laughing! This isn't funny!"

Cap'n Ron's House

Snapshot:
This deal was somewhat of a saga. We went to the home. We left the home. We went back to the home and dealt with all the characters involved. The whole process was not glamorous and none of REI is glamorous. It takes hard work and determination, just like anything else. But, I put up with this home, because I wanted to dive into this high-end neighborhood. I actually found this house while I was walking my dogs. It was more of a scouting mission. I wanted to see what the competition was doing. I happen to notice a real fixer in the neighborhood and wrote down the address. I mailed it. I got a call. I got a lead.

His name was Ron. The home was an inheritance. He owned the house with his two sister's. One of which lived in the home with her boyfriend; a unicyclist who liked to ride around wearing a top hat. We got the deal, despite this unique duo, and found plenty of surprises long after they had all left.

We had spent the last hour looking at Ron's house. Martha, his younger sister, was there. She talked about the beauty of the home. She said the ornamentation was a gift from God. I didn't think so. It was just old. It was worn out. Nothing in the house had been updated for 70 years. And the bathroom was completely gutted from a water leak. Before Martha said anything, I knew the work was done by someone who had no idea what they were doing. It was Martha's partner, who was a unicyclist by profession, was going to fix it himself. The driveway was a steep dive, too. It was shaped like a concrete slide. Go up? Go down? It doesn't matter. The bumper scrapes. We had room to bargain the price down and we thought we would try.

Ron was a man in his late 40's with dark hair and a style that was both his own and extremely outdated. He wore red shorts with a very short inseam. No matter the time or day, we got a good look at his hairy thighs.

We went outside. Ron, Chris and I stood on the stoop next to a mess of rusted chairs. I took a seat and Chris did too. Ron stood though. "So," Ron said. He lifted his right leg and balanced the sole of his foot on the chair. It was a familiar pose. One I had seen on Rum bottles. His shorts hiked up and tightened. Just as he asked what we thought it was worth, his shorts hiked up a little more. Was Ron not wearing underwear? I couldn't tell, but something didn't look right. Ron kept moving around. That's when I saw exactly what I didn't want to see. A small bulge of skin was popping out from between his legs. I froze. What the fuck? I thought. His balls are hanging out!

"So," Ron said again. "The price?"

"Uh," I said. "What – uh- what would you like for it?"

"Oh, I don't know." Ron leaned in a little. His shorts hiked up a little more. Oh god, I thought.

"Let me go back to the office," I said. "I'll put together some numbers. I don't want to fall short."

It took me a day or two, but I came up with a price. Chris Called Ron with the offer. "Yeah," Ron said. "I'll take three hundred thousand."

"Great," Chris said.

"About signing the papers, though," Ron said. I was standing next to Chris and it sounded like Ron's voice trailed off. Chris was shaking his head. "What?" He said. "Really? Are you serious?" Finally, he hung up the phone.

"So?" I asked.

"Well, he agreed to the number," Chris said. He took a deep breathe. "But, he wants to have a mediator there. At the signing."

"A mediator? Like, an attorney?"

"No. Like a mediator. Like a therapist to make sure his sisters don't fly off the handle."

I laughed. Whatever, I thought. Sure, I told Chris. When do we sign? "Friday night," Chris said. "At 7."

That week was busy and Friday came quickly. I hit the office. I hit the job sites. I had a couple of appointments. I even went home for a bit, before making my way to Ron's house. When I got there, Ron answered

the door. As expected, he was wearing short, red shorts and a Hawaiian

shirt. There was a mediator there. "Hi," he said. "I'm John. Martha's

therapist." Just like I had thought. The older sister, Lisa, was a stout

woman with gray, cropped hair. She offered me a seat at the table,

before she also sat down. "So," she said. "I just want to be clear. We have

another offer."

Another offer? Then what the hell am I doing here? I looked over

at Ron. He looked just as surprised as I did. "Okay," I said.

"For three hundred and twenty-five thousand dollars," she said.

"Is that right?" I said. "Well, what am I doing here? If you have an

offer that good. You should call them. In fact, you should call them right

now, and lock in that price. That price is too good to be true."

"Well," she said. "We haven't decided if we like the work they

do."

Bullshit, I wanted to say. She was bluffing. "I see," I said, and left it

there. I'm glad I did. Martha, the younger sister, became erratic about my

harmful nature and my potential desire to split the lot. I tried to explain

the lot is 5,000 square feet in size. The lot is zoned to be 5,000 and only

5,000, square feet in size. I couldn't split the lot. Even if I wanted to try, I couldn't. She wouldn't have it, though. "You have to promise," Martha said. "I want you to sign something."

"Sign what, exactly?" I asked.

"This says you promise not to split the lot," she said.

What the hell? I thought. I can't split the lot! Regardless, I would not split the lot. But, I smiled. I said, "Sure, Martha. I won't split the lot."

It seemed now that this nonsense was over, we could get down to business. And, we did. I agreed. I signed. They agreed. They signed. I handed over one of the signed contracts to Ron and he walked me outside. He apologized for his sisters. "I get it," I told him. "I knew there was no other deal. I knew the lot couldn't be split."

"Thank you," he said. "I'll call you when we've cleaned out."

"Thanks Ron," I said and left.

It took a couple weeks, but Ron was able to get his sister and the unicyclist out of the house. I took possession and my crew went to work soon after.

As soon as we began gutting the place, and pulling up old carpeting, we found some issues underneath. I knew we needed to look at the foundation and get under the house, and just as we did, the foundation buckled. I heard a crashing sound. I saw the crew scatter. I saw dust float up into a thick, churning cloud. "Oh shit," I muttered to myself. "What happened?"

Gerry, my project manager came running over. "I think the foundation is giving way," he said. "We need to check." What did we find underneath Ron's house? Thousands of little gold flakes. Are you serious? I thought. Now we have found gold?

Well, we thought we had. I took a sample to the local gold shop. An older-timer claimed it was the real deal. "Don't tell a soul," he said. "You might have a whole lot to sell."

I mailed off a different test sample. I wanted a chemical test done on the gold. It took a couple weeks, but the tests came back. Negative. It was fool's gold.

I picked up the phone and dialed Gerry's number. "Break's over," I said. "We've got a house to build."

The Cat Sh!t House

Snapshot:

The Cat Sh!t House was brought to our attention by a local probate attorney. He called our office and Chris wrote up a lead sheet to put on my desk. The deal had to do with two homes in the Woodstock neighborhood. What was the deal? Twin sisters. Each one had a house they needed to sell.

So, anyways, we looked at both homes. What we learned was this: the first twin sister had died. The second twin sister had been put in charge of liquidating the estate, but she had now become sick. So, the second twin's husband, the brother-in-law to the first twin sister, was trying to sell the first twin sister's house as well as his own.

Now, this is around 2010. We were new, but we weren't that new. We had completed quite a few renovations and we had our own steady crew in place. When you see what we were up against with each of these homes, you'll know why we passed on the first home. Our crew was loyal to our company and they were thankful for the steady work, and I didn't want anyone to quit on the job. So, all this is to say, the neighborhood was good, but the amount of work to be done was too much for the average crew.

We went to the appointment. We looked inside. We left. I never wore those clothes again.

On the phone, the brother-in-law seemed nice enough. "It's pretty bad," he said. "I think it'll be alright, though. The city has come and done a little clean up."

Sure, I told him. Don't worry. We've seen a lot. And we thought we had seen a lot.

We drove out to the appointment. The Woodstock neighborhood was getting a face lift at the time and it has become a much better place to live. We wanted to do more renovations in this area and we thought this was our ticket into the neighborhood.

The brother-in-law's name was Tim. He was a postal worker, he said. It was hard to deal with his wife being sick and grieving, and now he has to clear out her sister's house. He didn't want much for each home to begin with, so we thought we might be able to bridge the gap and make a deal.

"Let me take you inside," he said, and pulled out a set of keys.

We followed him inside and watched as he unlocked the door. It was then, as the door flung open, that I realized why he had been unspecific about the condition of the house. I could see from the doorway why he had kept insisting we come look at the place ourselves. I turned to Chris. I could tell he didn't know what to say.

"Come on in," Tim said.

We entered. The smell was like running into a wall. The scent of cat urine and feces had become a vaporous cloud that hung in the room. The sensation was what it must be like to walk through a home on fire, but our vision wasn't clouded by smoke. We could see. We could see alright. We just couldn't breathe.

I turned to Tim. I pointed at a huge pile of trash bags next to the door. I said, "Is that-?"

Tim cut me off before I could finish my question. "Yeah," he said. "That's what the city collected when they came in."

"But, it's not trash. It's-"

"Yeah," he said, interrupting me again. "It's cat droppings."

Droppings? It was 30 trash bags full of cat crap dug out of the carpet and the litter box. He said the Fire Department had come in after they took the first twin sister. They had to clear a path and they ended up bagging all this crap.

"Wow," I said. There was still trash everywhere.

As Tim showed us the rest of the house, I couldn't believe he wasn't more disgusted by the place. There was cat droppings on the kitchen counter and kitty litter was strewn across the carpet. I had to cover my nose with the collar of my shirt. Chris had his nose and mouth covered with a handkerchief. But Tim just strolled around and showed us different rooms inside. He seemed embarrassed, but that was it. And by the time we made it to the backyard, the scene had grown that much more surreal.

Up to this point, we hadn't seen any cats. Maybe we'd heard them meowing nearby. But Tim took us to the backyard, and that's when we saw them.

"So," he said. "This is the cat run." The cat run? I thought. The cat run? It was like a large chain kennel that fenced in the entirety of the backyard. The back yard was one giant cage and that cage had somewhere around 20 cats running around. There was a ramp that went up to the kitchen window. "Don't worry," he said. "The kitchen window is locked."

Tim explained he was trying to get rid of all the cats. There were 50 before. He had been able to get rid of half of the cats.

Tim motioned us back inside and said, "Let me show you the basement."

"Okay," I said. "If you have to..." I didn't want to see the basement. I didn't want to know. But Chris and I went down anyways and let Tim show us where another 10 or so cats had been living.

"These are the feral cats," he said. It was crazy and the room smelled even worse than the rest of the house. There was no window and no vent. These cats had been shitting and eating and pissing all over

the place. It was just a hot bed of ammonia.

"Alright," I said. I turned and stomped up the stairs. "That's it!

That's it!"

Chris and I stumbled outside and began to take long, deep

breathes. "The fresh air," Chris said. "It tastes so good."

"What's wrong?" Tim said. "Are you okay?"

"Yeah," I said. "I'm okay. But I don't know about you."

The "Golden Girls" House

Snapshot:
I first got wind of this lead through our online portal. One of the daughter's (I don't remember which one), contacted my company and asked for an appointment ASAP. We agreed and went to the home. Understand, this is back in 2010 when the Real Estate market wasn't so hot. Almost every deal was a good deal. But this deal was one of a kind. What do I mean? They wanted $95,000 for a home that was worn down, but still worth more. $95,000 wasn't even the land value. Needless to say, we quickly agreed to meet the family.

During our time building rapport, we found out the family has a daughter in Arizona, a daughter in Portland, a brother also In Portland, and the mother. The daughters were trying to sell the home and move the mother to Arizona. These older women, who had a brother on the loose, were feisty and flirty and with all that gold-digging attitude, we dubbed them the Golden Girls...

It's a bit of a twisted tale the way this deal went down. It was just Chris and I making our way to the Woodstock/Mt. Scott neighborhood. We didn't know the whole story then, but we soon found out.

The home was a small ranch house. One that is popular in the Portland Metro area. It was old, sure, but it wasn't worn to shit like some of the homes we had seen before. It was the neighborhood which called into question the home's value. I mean, if you stood on the Golden Girls porch, you could throw a rock in one direction and it would land onto the roof of a registered sex offender. You could throw a rock 90 degrees to the left and it would land inside the boarded up compound of a three-time convicted felon. Yeah, there wasn't much to look at, but in the last few years the neighborhood has seen much better times.

We knocked, but there was no answer. We could hear people inside. They were whispering. We knocked again. This time we heard the door open. An older woman about sixty answered the door. She cracked the door just enough to usher us in. "Hurry," she said. "Hurry, I don't want to give him a chance to come inside." We didn't know what she was talking about. Okay, we said and stepped inside.

Her name was Martha and she was the younger sister. Lisa, the older sister from Arizona, made sure to hug Chris. He tried to let go but she nuzzled in tight. Then, she hugged me too. "Thank God you're here," she said. She fiddled with the zipper to her track jacket and flicked her eyes. She was wearing a velvet track suit two sizes to small and made for a generation twenty years younger than her. She pulled down on the zipper and made sure I noticed all that tan, wrinkled cleavage.

"Nice to meet you?" I said, and took a seat opposite the sisters.

At first, I hadn't noticed the Mother sitting on the couch. I never did find out how old she was, but I'm sure, it was somewhere around 90. She didn't speak the entire time we were there. She didn't move. Martha and Lisa took control and made sure to tell us why *they* needed to sell the house. The story goes something like this: They have a brother. They had to kick the brother out of the house for a very specific reason. Now, first, remember this is 2010, and we were still deep into the dip of the recession. The brother had been out of work for a couple years. No real prospects for employment. He needed money. So, apparently, the mother had tried to kick the brother out several times because he was eating up all her food and somehow syphoning money out of her bank account. The sisters found out and came over to kick the brother out.

Okay, we said. Why? Why do you want to move mom to Arizona then? Why not kick him out and make sure he stays out?

"Well," Martha said. "You won't believe what we found in the crawlspace."

"What?" I said. "What did you find?"

Well, apparently, the brother had bought a headlamp, duct tape, rope, a shovel, and some Quicklime. All of this was wrapped in a sheet. "You know what that means?" Martha asked.

"He is gonna kill Mama," Lisa said.

"I see," I said. Now, I understood why she had ushered us in so quickly.

"So," Lisa said. She smiled and leaned closer. "What do you think of the house?"

To be honest, we hadn't even seen anything but the front yard and the living room. "Well," I said. "I can see you want to sell this thing quick, right?"

They nodded. I looked at the mother. I think I saw her nod, too.

"Okay," I said. "Considering you want to sell it fast. What do you think you would take?"

Without skipping a beat, Lisa said, "We'll take ninety-five."

Ninety-five? I thought. Ninety-Five thousand dollars? That's even less than the land value! "I see," I said. I kept a straight face. I hummed and I hawed and I shook my head at Chris.

"We need this," Martha said. "So we can bring Mama down to Arizona and buy us all a condo."

It was then, I understood what was going on. The sisters wanted to move mom to Arizona and use her money to buy *them* a condo *they* can live in. It just so happens, Mom will be there too. Mom will stock the fridge. Mom will pay the taxes. Mom's got a pot of gold and the Golden

Girls have a hand in that pot, too.

"I see," I said. "I think we've got a deal."

The Black Mold House

Snapshot:

The Black Mold House was brought to our attention by Kathy (not her real name). When she first called, she wasn't interested in selling the house she owned. Her and her siblings wanted to sell a home they had just inherited. We looked at the inherited home, but we passed. The inherited home wasn't worth what they were asking. Kathy then brought up her home. "Would you take a look at it?" she said. "We're thinking of selling in a few months." I said sure. We'll take a look.

Originally, she wanted $150,000. She made it sound like it was bigger and in better condition than it turned out to be. This might be a good deal, I thought. Well, in the end, I bought it for $95,000.

Before I get into the house we have named The Black Mold House, let me say that this house was a complete surprise inside. Almost always, our first impression of the outside is what we are going to see on the inside. Our first impression was wrong. Really, really wrong.

Kathy's home was just beyond 82nd Ave. This matters in Portland, OR. 82nd Ave. is the line. It's the line most renovators and house flippers won't cross unless it is a really, really good deal. I thought this home might be a really, really good deal. So, I went for it. I crossed the line.

My first hint should have been the shopping cart out front. Or, maybe the Astro Van resting up on bricks. But, the house itself didn't look that bad. From the outside, it needed some paint and lawn work. But, I thought, for $150,000 we could put some lipstick on it and do a quick and easy flip. They don't always go this way, but sometimes you get lucky.

I had Chris with me and we made our way to the front door. We knocked. A middle-aged man with a headband and sleeve-less t-shirt answered the door. "Sup dudes," he said, and waved us in. "Are you the real estate dudes?"

Chris looked at me. I looked at him. Does he really talk like that? I thought. "Yeah," I said. "My name is Tucker and this is Chris, my office manager." We shook hands. Headband made sure to squeeze tight. "Dave," he said. "My name is Dave."

I asked about his wife, Kathy, whom Chris had talked with on the phone. "Kathy!" He screamed. "Kathy! Get over here! Now!"

We heard Kathy shuffle through the house. The home had a strange lay out. It's like it went in a circle with the kitchen somehow in the middle. So, Kathy's footsteps came from some room in the corner and had to cross through another room before she could even meet us in the living room. She was a small woman with dark hair.

"Hi," she said. "I'm Kathy." We shook hands with Kathy, but before we could exchange niceties Dave shoved her off. "Let's take a look now, shall we?" Dave said. "Come on. Come on!"

Dave then started to guide us through the living room. It was a small space with a small wood burning stove in the corner. The entire house was maybe 900 square feet. But, the living room was full of stuff. It wasn't roof to ceiling with stuff like some of the others we have seen. It just had stuff in big piles. Blankets, for example. A pile of clothes in the other corner. A pile of chairs (yeah, I don't get it either) in the other corner. It was just random piles of stuff.

Somehow, Dave is providing a detailed tour of the living room. At some point, he motions toward the wood burning stove. "You don't have a furnace?" I ask. No, he explains, they do.

"Oh," I said. "It doesn't work?"

"No," Dave said. "It works."

"Why don't you use it?" Chris asked. I was curious, too. I wanted to know why someone wouldn't just run the heater they were using everything else that requires electricity.

Dave shrugged. He hummed and he hawed. He explained that it was too expensive to run the furnace. Too expensive? He had two young kids in the house. If it was me, I'd swallow that cost. They deserve to be warm. And yet, this wasn't my home. So, I put on my poker face and asked about the wood burning stove.

"It's cheaper," Dave explained. "But it dries out the air."

I told him that makes sense. That can happen. "So," he said. "I like to moisten the air."

That's when I noticed the old, hollowed out soup cans full of water. They were on top of the wood burning stove. The water was boiling and I started to notice the hot, wet heat filing the air. It was like a sauna. It was as if we were in a humid room in which the hot air had become trapped. "It's to help with the dry heat," Dave said. "I do this to clean out the air."

Is that alright? I wanted to say. Does this make sense? Everything did seem a bit moldy.

Chris and I followed Dave to the first bedroom in the house. "This is the kid's room," Dave said. He turned on the light and we couldn't believe what we saw. A thick brush of mold climbed the walls to the window. It was yellow and green and black. I couldn't believe the amount of mold right next to the children's bed. It must have climbed as high as our waist.

"It's probably seeping into walls," I said. "You might want to clean that."

"Clean what?" Dave asked.

I shook my head. I told him it was nothing. "Cool," Dave said. "Let me show you our room."

As Dave led us down the hall, we had to dodge more piles of clothes and blankets. I could now see they were starting to mold. It was the soup cans and the boiling water. Since they weren't using the central air system, there was no air being pushed in or out. It just stayed there. It just hovered in the small house.

What we saw in Dave's room was the worst deterioration we had ever seen. The mold was like a thick sludge. It was big and wet. The hues of yellow and green were that much brighter. No matter what else I saw, I knew we couldn't buy this house for the price they were asking. They wanted $150,000? This place is worth just a few bucks over the dirt! $150,000? How about $95,000?

Dave led us to the final room in the back. It was small and full of mold, too. Then he showed us the backyard, which was nothing but yellow grass and piled with more moldy blankets. At the end, I didn't actually want to put in an offer. But, back at the office, I had Chris tell Dave and Kathy we'd take their home for $95,000. I didn't think they'd take it. I didn't really care. This house was a hazard zone with all that black mold and I wasn't sure I wanted to deal with it.

In the end, I had Chris call them with my offer. I didn't expect anything. But, I was pleasantly surprised when they said yes. They would take $95,000.

Orange Soda & Candles

Snapshot:

Many of our leads come from our direct mail campaigns. Some of our leads come through our online website. This house happens to be one of those online leads. Based on the information we were given, the home sounded good. So, Chris made the call to set up the appointment. Based on the numbers and location, we thought we might have a good deal.

The home was two stories tall and somewhere around 1600 square feet. It was located in Inner Northeast. The owner, whom we deemed Powder, had said there was some light renovations inside the home. He also said he didn't have the time to finish the designs, so he wanted to unload the house and move onto the next project. Sure, we said. No problem.

Something I've learned in REI is that every investor has no idea what his or her lead is going to deliver. Distressed neighborhood? Sure. Wrecked home? So many. But, what type of people? You never, ever know. They may sound sane on the phone, but who you meet in-person is a strange surprise every single time. This house reinforced this point to no end. Remember, you think you know, but you don't. Be ready!

His skin was as white as paper. His skin had been shaved. Arms, legs, head – all shaved. And his eyebrows too! He had shaved his eyebrows, but we didn't know this at first. He had sunglasses on when he answered the door. He was like a vision of Powder. Yeah, *that* guy from *that* movie.

Before we met Powder, Chris and I first knocked on the front door, but no one answered. No problem, I thought, and rang the doorbell. Still, no answer. "Did you confirm this appointment?" I asked Chris. Yeah, he told me, he had confirmed the appointment that morning.

I shrugged. What was I supposed to do? I knocked again. No answer again. So, Chris and I stepped off the stoop and began peering in the front windows. I know its taboo, but I just wanted to peer inside the home and see what work Powder had done. I couldn't see much, though.

"Where is everything?" Chris asked.

"I don't know," I said. The home looked empty. No tables. No chairs. Nothing. It was hard to tell, though. The lights were off.

"He lives here?" I asked. Chris nodded.

"Where?" I asked. "It looks like there is nothing inside."

I went back to the stoop and tried the front door again. I knocked. Then, I knocked some more. Finally, we heard footsteps inside the home. That's when Powder answered the door and surprised us with his pale skin.

"Hey guys!" He said, and motioned us inside. "This is my home." He had a way of speaking that stretched out the last syllable of a sentence. An endless drawl, I suppose. It was a quirk, sure. One that matched the mess inside the house.

What Powder began to explain is that he was an accomplished designer. He was also a renovator. Oh, he was also a developer. By the look of this place, I didn't see it. The inside of the home was torn to pieces. The walls? Partly gutted. Tuffs of insulation were jutting out of random openings. The ceiling? Torn down to the base boards. And the design? There was none! I thought a tornado had touched down and ripped the place to shit.

As Powder began to show us the floor plan, he made sure we were careful not to step on any of the openings in the floorboards, because random slats were missing. "I didn't like those boards," he said. "They didn't look right."

"Okay," I said. I didn't know what he meant. Just replace the floor in sections, and don't rip the entire place apart. They didn't look right? What does he mean? I thought. I was about to ask, but Powder flipped up his sunglasses and that's when I first had a good look at his face. At first, I couldn't figure it out, but I knew something was missing. I'm sure I stared at Powder. I nodded as he spoke, but I wasn't listening. Then, I figured it out! No eyebrows!

This was a complete disaster. It was just chaos. And there was nowhere to sit down, except for a few lawn chairs circled together in the middle of the room. In the center of the chairs was a birdfeeder with a large candle. Around the candle was a mountain of cigarette butts.

Powder made sure to show us the fireplace. "This is my design," he said. The project was half-finished and didn't look much different from the original brick design. The kitchen, though, was another level of disaster. There were no appliances inside. Half of the cabinets had been replaced with a new set. The other half of the cabinets had been torn down. It just didn't make sense. So, I asked, what was his plan with this place?

"Well," Powder said. "My plan is to stay here, I guess, until I finish renovating the place."

"How long have you been at it?" Chris asked.

"I don't know," he said. "A few months, maybe. A year?"

That didn't help. But even if he had been ripping this home apart for a few months, anyone could see this project was going nowhere. I mean, what was one to do? It was such a mess, I wasn't exactly sure where to start cleaning it up. And just as I began to wonder if this was a lost cause, Powder suggested he show us the basement.

"Okay," I said, and Powder lead us to the back stairs.

The basement was a concave of leaking pipes and random piles of housewares. He had everything down there, and yet the entire floor was covered with an inch of water. "I'm going to finish this out," he said. "But first, I'm going to get steel beams inserted under the house and have it raised another 6 inches so the ceiling will be higher. It's a little short, I think."

I couldn't figure it out. He has big plans for this place, but he can't finish any of the small projects. He's going to raise the house? And, he still has his sunglasses on, though we're in the basement. I still can't get over the shaved eyebrows. This was all so weird. Why was this guy being so weird?

After we left the basement, we weren't done with the tour. We still had to look at the upstairs floor. Reluctantly, we took to the stairs. The stairwell was built at a strange angle. Some of the steps were missing.

This next scene is so bizarre, and I'm not even sure what happened. We went up the stairs. When we turned to ask Powder about the upstairs, he wasn't there. It seemed Powder had wandered off.

So, we took the tour ourselves. The first bedroom had nothing but a pair of blow-up mattresses. In the next room, we were startled to find a big, buff man at a card table typing on the computer. His hair was slicked back and dyed jet black. He smiled when he saw us. "Hey," he said, and went back to typing.

Chris and I took a few steps out of view. "Time to go," Chris said. "Please," I said, and hurried down stairs.

Outside, we found Powder on the stoop. I wanted to get the hell out of there, but I just wanted to know how much he was asking. It couldn't be much. The place was a wreck! So, I said, "What are you thinking about price?"

Before Powder could answer, his phone rang. "Hello?" He said. "Who is this?"

Powder looked at us. "Oh, hey... Yeah, they're still here."

"Are you going by the store?" He asked. "I need something."

What? I thought. What could you possibly need right now?

"Orange soda," Powder whispered into the phone. "And candles. Really big candles."

The Dirty Truth

If nothing else, this book is a series of snapshots, which, hopefully, share some humor and also shed some light on the investment side of Real Estate. Real Estate Investing is not glamorous. Every REI guru will tell you different. Don't believe it. Don't buy into it. Understand one thing: REI requires hard work and determination, and more than anything, it is a business. As the leader of that business, you have to get your hands dirty. There is no other way.

What do I mean, then? What is getting your hands dirty? Let me provide an example. Once, a probate attorney contacted our office to see if we were interested in a short sale. We looked at the paperwork. We looked at the numbers. We were interested and let the probate attorney know this. So, what did we find out when we went look at the house? The short sale was a disjointed foreclosure mess that kept being pushed out by the owner, who happened to also be an attorney! The owner was a drunk with a bisexual streak, who never wore a shirt. Don't ask me why.

We would agree to a price and some terms, and the next day, he'd call and say we took advantage of him while he was drunk. Sorry! I'd had to say. I didn't know you were drunk. So, in order to lock in this deal.

I had to take the guy to a liquor store and back. I had to hang out with him for a few hours while he did his laundry. I had to help him hang up his underwear. This is how I get my hands dirty. This I how I lock in my deals.

Sometimes, you can't lock in the deal. But, you have to try. You can only do this by going to the home in person. No virtual assistants. No little, yellow postcards. You, your service, and your personality. These are your basic tools.

Let's take another example. We get a call about a double lot in the first addition neighborhood of Lake Oswego. The price is right. The owner agreed to meet with us. So, we decided to take a look at the property. The house was in shambles. The owner had painted a rainbow pattern onto an old bed post and then nailed it above the door. Sure, I told her. It looks good. It's art, she said. Then, she said she would only to sell to us if we agreed to build an 8 room co-op with a shared bathroom. I had to listen and smile and not ask her if she was crazy. I had to bite my tongue. This is getting your hands dirty. These are the people you will meet. I couldn't close this deal, because I wasn't going to build a hippie commune. No problem. What's next?

There is the deal where the siblings fought and fought. Two brothers. One sister. The older brother, the irresponsible one, bullied the others, even though two out of three thought it was a good deal. What happens, then? An easy transaction turns into a difficult mess. In this one, Chris had to mediate. Chris had to play a therapist in order to help everyone communicate better. Again, I've had to get my hands dirty, and so has Chris. Once you're in it. It can be ugly, strange and bizarre. But the service we provide and the profit we make in return is well worth the effort.

So, what is The Dirty Truth? Real Estate Investing isn't glamorous. It isn't easy. It is real. There is money to be made. Get at it!

REI Survival Kit

Items to have on your person...

1. An extra person. Two is better than one. It is much safer. It is also easier to break the ice and build rapport. It will provide extra validity to the negotiations. Also, I believe 3 people is too many.

2. Business Card

3. Flash light

4. Cell Phone w/ Camera

5. Pocket Knife

6. It doesn't hurt to go to the appointment packing some heat...

7. A sense of humor and/or personality.

Items to have in your car...

1. Hand Sanitizer

2. Respirator/Face Mask/Air Spray

3. Blank Contract

4. Pen

.

www.ingramcontent.com/pod-product-compliance
Lightning Source LLC
Chambersburg PA
CBHW071003180526
45168CB00003B/1272